Everything You Need to Know About

TEEN
MOTHERHOOD

Motherhood demands a lot of time and patience.

• THE NEED TO KNOW LIBRARY •

Everything You Need to Know About

TEEN MOTHERHOOD

Jane Hammerslough

Series Editor: Evan Stark, Ph.D.

THE ROSEN PUBLISHING GROUP, INC.
NEW YORK

Published in 1990, 1992 by The Rosen Publishing Group, Inc.
29 East 21st Street, New York City, New York 10010

Revised Edition, 1992
Copyright © 1990, 1992 by The Rosen Publishing Group, Inc.

Manufactured in the United States of America.

Library of Congress Cataloging-in-Publication Data

Hammerslough, Jane.
    Everything you need to know about teen motherhood / Jane
Hammerslough. —Revised ed.
    (The Need to know library)
    Includes bibliographical references and index.
    Summary: Discusses practical aspects of becoming a teenage mother,
including what to do, how to do it, where to go for help, and what should
be known about such topics as budgeting and baby care.
    ISBN 0-8239-1459-3
    1. Teenage mothers—United States—Juvenile literature. [1. Teenage
parents. 2. Pregnancy.] I. Title. II. Series.
HQ759.4.H36   1990
306.58'6—dc20   89-39499
                                        CIP
                                        AC

Contents

Introduction

How can you give your baby the best start in life? How can you help your baby to stay healthy, before and after it is born? How can you make sure you and your baby have a good home and enough money? How will a baby fit into your own life, and how will it affect your own goals and dreams?

Everyone who decides to have a baby is faced with these questions. And teenagers who become parents have even greater concerns. It is important to think about these questions *before* your baby is born.

Having a baby is the biggest commitment you will ever make. Motherhood lasts for the rest of

your life. Maybe you are not sure that you want

that kind of responsibility. Talk with a teacher, guidance counselor, or someone at a health clinic about other choices. Books like *Everything You Need to Know About Teen Pregnancy* may also help.

Having a baby changes your life forever. It can be difficult at times. Deciding to become a mother means that you become responsible for another person's life. Babies are totally dependent on their parents, and have a lot of needs. Caring for these needs takes up a lot of time, and can be very tiring. It can test your patience. When you become a mother, you will have less time for your friends and yourself.

Having a baby can also be very rewarding. It is a very special experience. Most mothers feel great love for their babies, even though taking care of them is a lot of hard work.

Teenagers who decide to become mothers have special needs. If you are pregnant, good nutrition and medical care are especially important because you are still growing. This book tells how you can take care of yourself while you are pregnant and after your baby is born.

If you are a mother already, this book can help you learn how to give your baby the best care. It can also help you think about your own future.

Being late with your period could mean pregnancy.

Chapter 1

New Responsibilities

Lori and Mark never thought much about pregnancy. It was the kind of thing that happened to other people. It was like being in a plane crash, or winning the lottery. But lately Lori feels sick in the morning. Her breasts are hard, and sore. And it's been more than two months since her last period.

A trip to a family-planning clinic agrees with what Lori suspected: she is pregnant. She feels scared, angry, confused, and lonely. Because of her religious beliefs, Lori will not have an abortion. She also doesn't know if she could give up the baby growing inside of her.

Every day in the United States, more than three thousand teenage girls find out that they are pregnant. That adds up to more than a million teenage pregnancies each year. Some of these are planned. Most are not. Most girls who find out they are pregnant are like Lori. They feel partly happy. But they are also upset, afraid, and unsure of what to do. Each can learn how to be the best mother possible.

Making the Right Decisions

Having a baby is one of the biggest changes that will ever happen in your life. The choice to raise a baby is a lifetime decision. It is important to think about how that decision will affect you now and in the future.

Most teenage girls become pregnant by accident. But some get pregnant on purpose. Some teenage girls believe that having a baby will make them adults. Others believe that a baby will solve problems with their parents or boyfriends. Some think that having a baby will be all fun and no work. These girls are almost always disappointed. Becoming a mother does not solve your problems.

It is important to know the facts about motherhood before you have a baby. Talk over your thoughts with a friend, parent, teacher or school counselor. This will help you make the best decisions for yourself and for your baby. Learning about the responsibilities of parenting can help you take control of the situation. It will also help you make the right decisions now and in the future.

Sometimes teenage girls become mothers without *taking control* of that decision. Taking control means learning about being a parent. It means thinking about the future. It means sorting out your feelings to decide what is best for you and your baby. Even if you become pregnant by accident, you can take control. You can think about how you feel now and learn the facts about being a mother.

Changing Needs

You have special needs when you are pregnant. You have different needs once your baby is born. A baby also has many needs. It is important to understand these needs.

When you are pregnant your body changes. You need to eat certain foods to help your baby grow properly. You also need special medical care. It is important for you and your baby to stay healthy during your pregnancy.

You and a baby need a safe, secure place to live. You need money to pay for a baby's expenses. You may also need child care so that you can go to work. Good child care can be expensive. Your financial needs change when you become a mother.

Almost all expectant and new mothers need personal support. Pregnancy can make you moody and upset, no matter how happy you are about having a baby. Being a new mother can be scary. It will help if you can talk about your worries and needs to someone who cares. You can get personal support from your family, the baby's father, and your friends.

You may also have needs that you can't talk about with your family or friends. Sometimes it is easier to talk with a school guidance counselor, a teacher, or a counselor at a family-planning clinic.

While you are pregnant, it is important to think about being a mother. Consider these sources of support:

○ **Your Family**   If you are a single parent, will your parents let you and your child live at home? Will they give you money for things the baby needs? Can they help you when you need help? It is important to think about whether your family can offer support.

Sometimes your parents want you to raise a baby because they want a grandchild. But you must think of yourself and your baby first. Can you and your parents agree on the best way to raise a child? Will you feel trapped? Will you have trouble moving out or marrying in the future? If something happened to your parents, would you be able to take care of a child yourself?

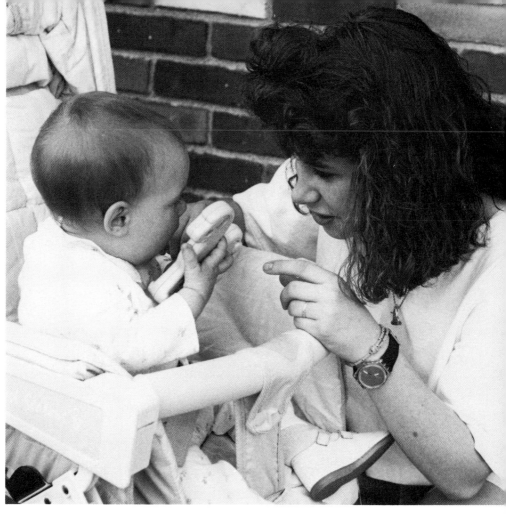

The choice to have a baby is a lifetime decision.

○ **The Father** Perhaps the father of the baby is
the most important person in your life right
now. Maybe he is no longer part of your life.
Either way, you should find out if he is willing
to support your decision.

You may be able to get emotional support
from the father. He may be able to "be there"
for you. Maybe he can also provide money for
things the baby needs. You will probably know
if the father is willing to stand by you. It is
important to be realistic. How much money will

you need? How much is the father able, or
willing, to give?

Sometimes the father thinks you ought to keep
the baby. But he may not be willing to accept
the emotional and financial responsibility of
being a parent. He might think that being a
father makes him more macho. He may think
being a father proves he is a man. But is he
thinking about you? Is he thinking about the
baby, and the baby's future?

○ **Objective Support** Getting support from
someone who isn't involved in your decision can
be very helpful. You can talk to a teacher or
counselor about your feelings. They won't judge
you. They may help you think about things
more clearly. You don't have to tell anyone in
your family you are talking to an "outsider"—
it's your own business.

○ **You** You can be a source of support for
yourself. Be honest about your own desires,
fears, and choices. If the father is not part of
your life, how do you feel about being a single
parent? About your child growing up without a
father? How do you feel about your family
taking part in raising your child? Or *not* taking
part? You can help yourself by thinking about
these things.

Becoming a mother creates special needs. The
purpose of this book is to help you find answers to
those needs.

Chapter 2

Preparing for Motherhood

Your body goes through many changes when you are pregnant. You are important to your baby before it is even born. When you decide to become a mother, it is important to get medical care as soon as possible. You can go to a local health clinic for care.

Prenatal Care

Prenatal means "before birth." Prenatal care is very important for your own health and the health of the baby. This means going to see a *midwife* or a doctor who delivers babies as soon as you can. This special kind of doctor is called an *obstetrician*. A midwife is not a doctor, but she is trained to care for expectant mothers and to deliver babies.

Pregnancy lasts for nine months. A midwife or obstetrician will usually see you once a month for the first seven months. After that, you will go every two weeks. At the very end of your pregnancy, you will go each week.

You will give information on your medical history at your first visit. This will probably be your longest visit. The doctor or midwife will also examine you. He or she will check your lungs, heart rate, breasts, weight and blood pressure to make sure you are healthy. You will also give blood and urine samples. At the visit you will learn your *due date*. That is the time when the doctor expects that your baby will be born.

Later exams take less time. Your weight and blood pressure will be checked at each visit. The doctor or midwife will also measure you to make sure your baby is growing well. After about the fourth month, you may be able to listen to your baby's heartbeat.

How You May Feel

Pregnancy lasts about forty weeks. Each three-month period is called a *trimester*. There are three trimesters in each pregnancy.

Being pregnant is a big change for your body. You may feel different than you usually do. Here are some ways you might feel different during each trimester.

The baby's father may want to help with preparing for the baby.

First Trimester (Months One–Three)

o Sleepy or tired
o Feeling sick to your stomach (nausea), vomiting ("morning sickness")
o Indigestion or heartburn
o Breast changes—fullness or tenderness
o Need to use the bathroom (urinate) very often
o Constipation
o Headaches
o Dizziness
o Food cravings (or dislikes)

You may also feel irritable or moody. You may feel like crying one minute, and happy the next. All of these feelings are normal during the first trimester.

Second Trimester (Months Four–Six)

o Less sleepy or tired
o Much less nausea and vomiting
o Indigestion or heartburn
o Enlarged breasts, less tenderness
o Mild swelling of hands and feet
o Headaches
o Better appetite
o Veins appear on legs (varicose veins) or hemorrhoids (piles) develop in the rectum (backside)
o Aches in abdomen (it is stretching for the baby)
o Fetal movement (the baby is now called a *fetus;* it is growing, and you may feel it moving)

○ Backache
○ Dizziness
○ Leg cramps
○ Itchiness

You may continue to feel irritable. Or you may begin to feel better. You may also forget things. During this trimester, your shape changes. You begin to "show." You may become clumsy as you get bigger.

Third Trimester (Months Seven–Nine)

○ Tiredness
○ Movement of baby (fetus)
○ Achiness
○ Constipation, heartburn, indigestion

Regular medical check-ups during pregnancy are important.

○ Headaches and dizziness
○ Leg cramps; mild swelling of legs, feet or hands
○ Some shortness of breath; trouble sleeping
○ Itchiness
○ Varicose veins, hemorrhoids
○ Backache, leg cramps
○ Changes in appetite

During this time you may continue to feel forgetful. You may also dream about having a baby. You may feel excited, scared, restless or bored with being pregnant.

You may feel many of these things during each trimester. Or you may feel few of these things. It is normal either way.

Your prenatal visits are a time to ask your doctor or midwife questions about your pregnancy. Make a list of questions before you go in. Call your doctor or midwife if you begin to bleed or get a high fever. You should also call even if you just think something might be wrong.

What to Eat When You are Pregnant

The food that you eat when you are pregnant is very important for your health and for your baby. This is especially important for teenage mothers. Teenagers are still growing. Your baby needs good food to develop properly. Your body also needs special *nutrients* (food elements—protein, vitamins, etc.) to be healthy.

Eating good, fresh foods during pregnancy is important. Pregnancy is not a time to diet. You and your baby need more good, fresh food to develop. But you cannot eat anything you like just because you are "eating for two." Junk food will only make you fat. It will not help you or your baby.

You should gain weight slowly and steadily when you are pregnant. It is best to gain between twenty and thirty pounds. Don't starve yourself because you feel "fat." Being fat and being pregnant are very different.

You can give your baby the best start by following these suggestions on what to eat:

Protein Foods

You should have *four servings* of protein foods a day. They help your baby grow. Each of these is one serving:

  3 8-oz. cups of milk
  ¾ cup of cottage cheese, 2–3 oz. of hard cheese
  2 eggs
  2–3 oz. of tuna, chicken, turkey, fish, lean beef,
    pork, veal, lamb, liver, or shellfish
  1 cup of black or other dried beans
  5 oz. of tofu
  4 tablespoons of peanut butter

It is best to have fresh, homemade food. Avoid fast food as much as you can. Broiling or baking is

Breakfast

Lunch

better than frying. Good high-protein snacks include nuts and whole-grained baked goods.

Calcium-Rich Foods

These foods help your baby's bones develop. They also help keep your teeth in good shape. Have *four servings* every day of these foods:

8 oz. cup of milk, 1¾ cups cottage cheese or 1 cup yogurt (this can also count as part of your daily protein)

2 oz. of hard cheese

3–4 oz. of canned salmon, mackerel or sardines with bones

Snack

Dinner

2–3 tablespoons sesame seeds

⅔ cup of collard greens

1¼ cup of fresh kale, mustard or turnip greens

1½ cups of broccoli

2–3 tablespoons molasses

2–3 oz. almonds

Vegetables and Fruits

Have *two or three servings* a day. One should be raw:

    ¾ cup of apricots, mango, papaya, peaches, or pumpkin

    ⅔ cup of beet, turnip or collard greens or broccoli

½ cup of carrot, fresh lettuce or spinach

½ cup of squash, sweet potato, swiss chard

You also should have at least one or two servings
of the following each day:

1 whole apple, pear, or banana, ½ cup berries,
    cherries, or grapes

½ cup green beans, asparagus, brussel sprouts,
    mushrooms, potato or zucchini

If possible, eat fruits and vegetables raw. Cooking
can destroy vitamins.

Whole Grains and Carbohydrates

These foods give you energy. Have *four to five
servings* daily:

1   slice whole-wheat bread

½ cup cooked rice

½ cup cooked cereal, such as Wheatena

½ cup whole-grain ready-to-eat cereal (like
    Shredded Wheat)

½ cup cooked pasta

During your pregnancy you will need more iron.
Eating dried fruits, liver, beef, and spinach can
give you more iron. You also need Vitamin C.
Have a glass of citrus juice (orange or grapefruit)
or a fresh orange, strawberries, grapefruit,
tomatoes, or a green pepper every day.

Your body also needs small amounts of fat each
day. You can get this in oil, butter, margarine,
mayonnaise or cream. Don't overdo it. You don't
want to gain too much weight.

Remember to drink plenty of liquids when you are pregnant. The best ones are water, juice and herbal teas.

What to Avoid When You are Pregnant

Everything that you take when you are pregnant can affect your baby. To make sure you give him or her the best chance to be healthy, you should avoid these things:

○ **Smoking** If you smoke, try to quit. If you can't quit, cut down. Smoking causes low birth weight in babies.

○ **Drugs** Drugs can hurt your baby. It is not fair to a baby to take drugs while you are pregnant. This includes marijuana, cocaine, crack, uppers, downers, or anything else you might consider taking for fun. It also includes over-the-counter medications. Even aspirin can hurt your baby. *Always* check with your doctor or midwife before you take anything.

○ **Caffeine** Too much caffeine is bad during pregnancy. Limit yourself to one cup of tea or coffee a day, or one soft drink or soda that contains caffeine.

○ **Alcohol** Alcohol is dangerous during pregnancy. If you drink alcohol during pregnancy it can harm your baby. The baby may be born with mental problems. Or physical problems.

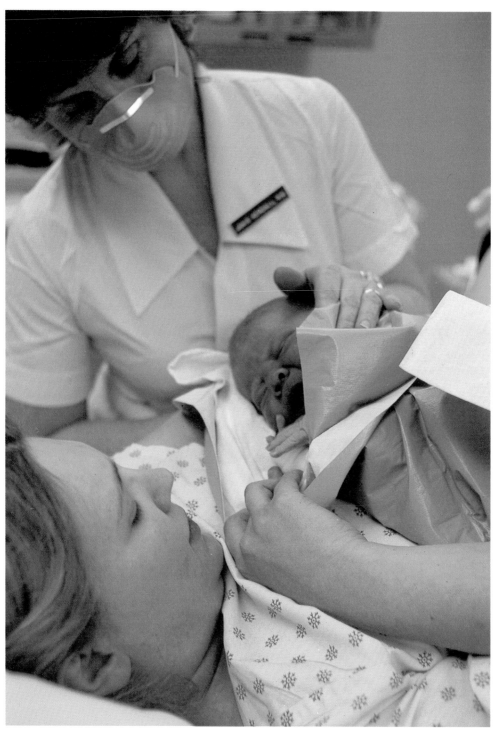

Holding the newborn baby is an exciting moment for the new mother.

Chapter 3

Having a Baby

The process of having a baby is called *childbirth*. It can be intense or exciting. It can also be scary. It is best if you understand what happens to your body during childbirth.

Many doctors and midwives believe that relaxing during childbirth is important. You can learn to relax in prepared childbirth classes. One type of class is called *Lamaze* (Lah-mahz).

In Lamaze classes you learn ways of breathing that help you relax. You and a "coach" practice together. Your coach can be the baby's father, someone in your family, or a friend. Some classes offer discussion groups, films on giving birth, and visits to the hospital where you deliver. Ask your obstetrician or midwife about Lamaze classes.

Stages of Childbirth

Labor

The first part of childbirth is called *labor*. It is
called labor because it is hard work. During labor
your *uterus* prepares to give birth. Your uterus is
where your baby has lived for the last nine months.
Your *cervix* is the entryway from the uterus to the
birth canal. During labor your cervix opens up.
The doctor or midwife will say that you are *dilating*
(die-lating).

Labor occurs in three stages. The first is called
early labor.

Early labor is the longest and least intense phase
of labor. It can last from a few hours to several
days. During early labor you will feel *contractions*.
Contractions feel like squeezes inside of you. They
last thirty to forty-five seconds. You may feel some
cramps, indigestion, or diarrhea. You may also
have "bloody show," a pink discharge from your
vagina. When contractions are five minutes apart,
you should go to the hospital.

Active labor is the second phase. This phase can
last two to four hours. Contractions are stronger
and more frequent. This means your body is

preparing for delivery. Breathing exercises can help you relax during this phase. You may feel pain or dizziness.

Transitional labor is the last and shortest phase of labor. Your contractions are two to three minutes apart and become very strong. They last for sixty to ninety seconds. Transitional labor can last from fifteen minutes to an hour. You may feel very tired and find it hard to relax.

Pushing and Delivery

Pushing and delivery is the second part of childbirth. It begins when your cervix is open wide enough for a baby's head. This part of childbirth can last anywhere from ten minutes to three hours.
You will continue to have contractions during this stage. Your obstetrician or midwife will tell you when to push. Sometimes pushing can be very intense. Usually a baby's head comes out first. Pushing the baby out is called delivery.

Delivery of Placenta

The final part of childbirth is delivery of the *placenta*. The placenta is where your baby lived inside the uterus. You push out the placenta. It takes any time from five minutes to half an hour.

Caesarian Births

Sometimes a baby must be delivered with surgery. This is called a *caesarian* section delivery. During a caesarian the doctor makes an *incision* (a cut) and removes the baby surgically through your abdomen. Anesthesia (an-es-the-sia) makes you go to sleep before the procedure.

Sometimes you have a caesarian delivery because the baby is in trouble. It must be delivered very quickly. Sometimes it is better for your own health to have a caesarian.

Postnatal Care

Postnatal means "after birth." You will receive post-natal care in the hospital after you have given birth.

Many new mothers are very happy and tired right after delivery. In some hospitals you will be able to hold your baby right away. In others the baby will be taken away for a while. In any case, you will be able to see your baby soon.

You may stay in the hospital for a day or more after having your baby. With a caesarian you will stay in the hospital longer. You will be examined each day by your obstetrician or midwife. You may feel very sore from having your baby.

Chapter 4

The First Months

Some new mothers believe that their babies are beautiful from the very beginning. Others aren't so sure. Many new babies look wrinkled or skinny. Your baby might not look the way you expected it to look. After a few weeks, most babies begin to fill out and look better.

You may be very tired for the first few days after you give birth. It is important to get plenty of rest while you are in the hospital and during the first few days that you are home. Having someone to help you with the baby and housework in the beginning is always a good idea if it is possible.

Soon after you give birth, you may feel sad or anxious. You may feel like crying, even if you are happy about having a baby. These feelings are

31

A new mother will need time to care for her baby. She may have less time to spend with friends.

called *post-partum depression.* Many new mothers have these feelings. Sometimes they seem to happen for no reason. These feelings are normal, and usually go away in a few weeks.

Caring for an Infant

Taking care of a newborn means doing many different tasks. Feeding, bathing, diapering, and holding are just a few of the things mothers need to know. These things are not hard to learn, but they do take a little practice.

Holding Your Baby

Always support your new baby's head when you hold him or her. A newborn's neck is not strong.

Newborn babies have a soft spot on the top of their heads called a *fontanel.* Be careful of this soft spot when you are handling the baby. After about a year, the fontanel becomes hard.

Feeding Your Baby

Babies need to eat often, especially in the first few weeks of life. You will need to decide how you want to feed your baby. Most mothers can choose between breast feeding and bottle feeding. Many mothers do some of each.

Breast feeding is the most natural method of feeding because your body is designed especially for it. You produce milk that is always pure and at the right temperature. And your milk contains the nutrients a baby needs. There is nothing to buy. It is all there, ready when needed. Your milk also contains your *antibodies*. Antibodies are natural chemicals in your body that protect the baby from certain infections.

When you breast feed, you can continue with your pregnancy diet. You should drink plenty of liquids as well. Breast feeding burns many calories.

Bottle feeding means giving a baby a bottle filled with *formula*. Today, most mothers use prepared formulas that are meant to be similar to mother's milk. You can buy formula in most drugstores and supermarkets. Bottle feeding is much more expensive than breast feeding, and it can take time to prepare.

Some new mothers decide to breast feed for a few months. Later, they use a combination of breast feeding and formula feeding. Doing this can help you have the advantages of both methods.

Both breast feeding and bottle feeding can help you to *bond* with your baby. Bonding is a feeling of closeness. It makes a baby feel loved.

Feeding Schedules

In the past, mothers fed their babies according to a schedule. But some babies need to eat more often than others. Now, most mothers feed their babies *on demand*, when they seem hungry.

A baby may cry after eating because it needs to burp. Babies swallow a lot of air by sucking when they feed. All this air can hurt their stomachs. Hold the baby upright against your chest and gently rub or pat its back.

Sleeping

Newborn babies sleep a lot of the time. After you feed and burp your baby, it is a good idea to put him or her in a crib. That way the baby will get used to the idea of sleeping after eating.

Diapers

A few days after your baby is born, it will produce a very dark stool (bowel movement) called *meconium*. This is normal.

Most babies have a very dark part of their *umbilical cord* still attached at their belly buttons for

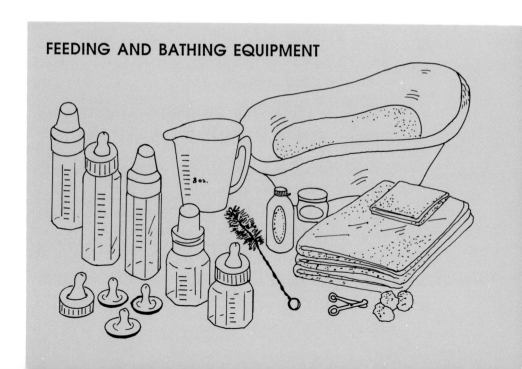

FEEDING AND BATHING EQUIPMENT

a few weeks after birth. It does not look very
pretty, but this is also normal. After a few weeks,
the cord will dry up and fall off.

Sometimes babies cry because their diapers are
wet or cold. Wet diapers can also cause diaper
rash. Diaper rash can be painful for your baby. It
is best to check and change diapers often.

Most mothers choose between cloth diapers and
disposables. Cloth diapers are easy to use with
diaper covers and can be picked up, washed, and
delivered by a diaper service. Disposable diapers
can be very convenient but they are expensive.
They also create much garbage that strains the
environment.

Baths

You can give your baby a bath every day. At
first it can be scary to give a baby a tub bath,
because the tub is very slippery. You can start with
sponge baths for a few weeks and work up to tub
baths.

You can give a bath in a dishpan or small tub in
a warm place. The water should be about body
temperature and feel comfortably warm. Before you
start, set a towel aside for drying the baby.

Support the baby's back and head with one arm
while you soap the baby with the other. Use only
an inch or two of water until you get used to giving
baths. You only need to wash the baby's scalp once
or twice a week.

Chapter 5

Care for You and Your Baby: Questions and Answers

After a few months, you will get to know your baby. You will become more confident about taking care of your baby. You will start to learn what it likes and needs.

But all new mothers have questions about their babies. Here are some of the questions that new mothers often ask:

Help! My baby won't stop crying! What should I do?

In the beginning, some babies don't cry much at all. Some cry often. You can try feeding the baby, changing it, turning it over, singing to it, or just holding it. Doing these things may help. Sometimes, though, a baby just won't stop crying.

Constant crying can be caused by *colic*. Colic causes sharp pains in your baby's intestines after eating. You can tell the difference between hungry crying and colic. A baby who is hungry cries before eating, not after. Colic may be relieved by burping the baby, rocking it gently, rubbing its back, or giving it a pacifier. Nobody is sure what causes colic.

Colic can make you mad when nothing you try seems to help. Fortunately, it usually goes away when the baby is around three months old.

Can I spoil my baby by holding it too often?

No. In the first few months, it's important to hold your baby often. Holding your baby and talking to it lets the baby know that you love it. The baby begins to learn that you will be there when it needs you.

My baby is driving me crazy, and I feel trapped. What should I do?

If you feel upset, it is always best to talk to somebody about it. Talk to a counselor, a friend, or your family about your feelings. If you feel very angry toward your baby, count to 10. See if you can find a babysitter and go out by yourself for an hour. If you can take time to calm down you won't take your frustration out on your baby.

Your baby is helpless and doesn't understand that its crying may upset you. Child abuse is a very serious problem. **Never, never hit an infant for any reason.** Hitting your baby is child abuse.

It is important to keep baby clean and comfortable with regular baths.

Medical Questions

Since I gave birth, I've been bleeding. Is this normal?

Yes. For a week or two after birth, new mothers discharge *lochia*, which is similar to having your period. If heavy bleeding lasts longer than that, speak to your health care practitioner.

Do I need to see a doctor after I have my baby?

Yes. Arrange to see your obstetrician, midwife, or gynecologist for a check-up six weeks after delivery. At this time you will be given an internal exam. Pregnancy is possible during these early

Always keep the pediatrician's phone number handy.

weeks. You may want to discuss birth control with your healthcare professional at the time of your check-up. It's important to plan when and if you want another child.

When should I take my baby to the doctor?

Your baby will need to see a doctor two weeks after birth and every month or so for the first year. A doctor who cares for infants and young children is called a *pediatrician*. Well-baby care is important to your baby's health. Your baby will need a series of shots. These shots protect a baby from diseases. The doctor will also check your baby's weight and length. Later, your baby will still have regular check-ups, but less often.

Ask your pediatrician questions about your baby's health and development. If you are concerned about something, talk to your doctor.

My baby has a rash. What should I do?

Call your pediatrician. Some rashes are common, like diaper rash. Rough or bumpy red patches in the diaper area are a sign of diaper rash. It can be caused by wetness. If there is a rash, do not use plastic pants, which keep in moisture. Wash the area carefully and rinse soap off twice with clear water. (If left on the skin, soap can make the problem worse.) Other kinds of rashes may be a sign of allergies or illness, and should be checked.

Why does my baby's scalp look dirty, even though I wash it?

Your baby may have *cradle cap,* which is a crusty irritation of the scalp. Cradle cap is very common in the early months of life. Daily washing with soap and water may help. The condition disappears after a few months.

What should I do if my baby has diarrhea?

A baby's intestines are sensitive for the first couple years of life. Bowel movements may be loose especially if you are nursing. Remember, you can always call your pediatrician with any questions or concerns you may have.

My baby is cranky and keeps pulling on both ears. Is it okay?

Call your pediatrician as soon as possible. Your baby may have an ear infection. This is common in infants and painful for them. Your doctor can give you medicine to make your baby feel better. The medicine can prevent damage to your baby's hearing.

Emergencies

It is a good idea to keep a list of important phone numbers by your phone. In an emergency, you will save time if all your numbers are in one place. You should call your pediatrician *immediately* if your baby:

- is vomiting with great force more than once a day
- eats any drug, chemical, or object by mistake
- seems to be having trouble breathing or is choking
- seems to be sick or have a temperature

Development

It is always a good idea for parents to pay attention to their baby's physical development. That means watching to see that your baby is alert, can focus its eyes, and has some coordination. It is important to remember that all babies develop at their own rate. Each baby will have its own schedule for development. The list that follows will give you an idea about some of the things most babies do in the first six months. If your baby does not do all these things it is no cause for alarm. Just keep paying attention. If you become concerned, you should tell your doctor what you're worried about.

Baby's First Six Months: What Happens When?	
AGE IN MONTHS	DEVELOPMENT
1	Grasps finger; pushes out arms and legs, reponds to touch
2	Follows movement with eyes; hands open more; shows emotions, soothed by voice and touch
3	Cries less, smiles; can lean on elbows while on stomach
4	Can hold onto objects, puts them in mouth; laughs; can lift head
5	Rolls from stomach to back; smiles and babbles for attention; head steady; enjoys touching and tasting objects
6	Sits with support; turns head; makes many sounds to express excitement, delight or fear; can hold bottle

Friends or relatives may have baby clothes their babies have outgrown.

Chapter 6

Seeing Yourself As a Mother

Becoming a mother causes many changes. It often changes the way you see yourself. It changes the way others see you. Having a baby will affect relationships with your friends, and with the father of your baby. It will affect your relationship with your family.

Will you continue to live with your parents after the baby is born? Think about your family. Do you get along well with your parents? Do they treat you like you are still a child? When you become a mother, your role within your family changes. You are no longer only your parents' child. You have become a parent, with responsibilities of your own. Sometimes that can be very hard for your parents to accept.

Your friendships will probably also be different after you have a baby. Becoming a mother takes a lot of time. It is tiring. You probably won't spend as much time with your friends as you used to. Your interests change. The things that are important to you may also change. You will have responsibilities that are different from those of most teenagers. You should consider how your role will change.

When you become a mother, the way you and the baby's father get along may also change. You might become closer, or you might find that the only thing you have in common is the baby. You may have no relationship at all, especially if he didn't want you to have the baby. It is important to think about this relationship. You need to be realistic about what your life will be like after the baby is born.

How do you see yourself in relation to your family, friends, and the baby's father? How do you see yourself as a mother? Does your family approve or disapprove of your becoming a mother? Do you like to spend lots of time with your friends? Once the baby is born, you won't have as much time to socialize. How do you think you'll get along with the father of your baby? Raising a child changes your life forever. But being prepared by thinking about the changes helps. It makes it easier to go from being a teenager to being a teenage mother.

Chapter 7

Practical Decisions

Your decision to become a mother involves practical choices. Practical choices are where you'll live, how you will support yourself and your baby, how to continue your education, where to find child care, and others.

Toni

When Toni learned she was pregnant, her boyfriend Carl wanted to quit school and get married. He thought they should move out of their parents' houses and raise the baby together. But Toni wasn't so sure.

She loved Carl, and thought that she wanted to spend the rest of her life with him. But she always thought that they should get married later. She thought they should finish high school and then work for a few years. Toni used to daydream about the beautiful wedding they would have, and the cute apartment they would share—in the future. Now, that didn't seem possible.

Carl thought she was being silly. He argued. If she loved him, he said, she would be willing to do anything. She would move anywhere. Toni felt guilty. But she thought he was not being realistic. And neither of them wanted to live with their parents.

Toni decided to talk with Ms. Collins, a guidance counselor at school. Ms. Collins gave her some useful ideas for figuring out what to do.

○ Toni and Carl should decide where they want to live. Then they need to find out how much apartments there cost to rent. Ms. Collins suggested looking in the classified section of the newspaper. There they could find out what was available. Then they could go together to look at places to live.

○ They should also look in the classified section for job listings. Carl and Toni need to know what kinds of jobs are available to people like them, without high school diplomas or specific skills.

○ They should find out about day care, and figure out how much it would cost. Ms. Collins told Toni about suggested school-age motherhood

It is helpful to get information about jobs, child-care and housing, before making decisions.

programs. In those programs, girls like Toni can finish their education and take care of their babies at the same time.

It is best to find out what things cost *before* the baby is born. Then you can make the best decision. When you have the facts, your feelings become more clear and realistic.

Where You'll Live

You and your baby must have a safe, secure place to live. Some teenage girls who are pregnant can choose where they want to live. Some have only one alternative. Reaching a decision on where you and your baby will live can sometimes be tough.

To make the best choice, you might ask yourself questions like these:

○ Is it a good place for an infant? Is there enough space, light, and quiet?

○ Do you get along with the people you will live with? Will they take advantage of you?

○ What kind of contribution will you be able to make to the household? If need be, will you be able to work to help out with expenses?

○ Will someone else at home be available at times to help you take care of the baby?

Your Expenses

Becoming a mother involves many expenses. A crib or a stroller is a one-time expense. Other expenses like food and clothing continue. To give your baby the best start in life, learning about these expenses is important.

Many teenage mothers have problems with money. Most live at a low income level. Some public assistance is available. Call your local Department of Social Services for more information on getting welfare. You can also call them about receiving food stamps.

It is better to have other sources of income, if possible. It is also best to finish high school as soon as you can. People with high school diplomas have a much better chance of earning a higher income.

The demands of being a teenage mother are great. It is not easy to go to school and take care of a baby. It is even more difficult to try to earn money at the same time.

It helps to ask yourself questions like these:

○ Is the baby's father able to help out with these expenses? Is he willing to pay?
○ Can your parents or the father's parents help you and the baby with money?
○ Have you looked into education programs for school age mothers? These can often make finishing high school much easier. Call your local Board of Education.

Child Care

If you work you will probably need child care.

○ Ask your family, friends and neighbors if they know anyone. If you find someone this way, make sure you trust them with your baby.
○ Call the Agency for Child Development in your area to find out about government-run day care programs.
○ Share baby-sitting with a friend who also has a baby.

Monthly Budget

Expenses for:	Cost
Rent	
(deposit or security)	
Electricity	
Heat	
Telephone	
(hook up)	
Child Care	
Food	
Clothing	
Laundry	
Health Care	
Transportation (buses, etc.)	
Social Life (movies, restaurants)	
Other Expenses	
1.	
2.	
3.	
4.	
Total needed:	

Create a budget by making a list of your monthly expenses.

Chapter **8**

Making a Budget

Think about the things you will need for a baby now and in the future. Having a budget gives you a good idea of how much money you need. It helps you decide which expenses are most important. Figure out how much each thing costs and put it down on paper.

When you have a baby, some expenses continue, some you only pay for once. Which of the following expenses will you need to pay for when you are a mother? Which are necessities? Which are optional?

Basic Expenses

Apartment (security deposit and monthly rent)
  Heat
  Electricity
  Laundry
Telephone (hook-up and monthly charges)
Food (for self and baby)
Clothing (for self and baby)
Child care
Health care and insurance (for self and baby)
Transportation (buses, etc.)
Car (payments and insurance)
Social life (movies, restaurants, etc.)
Savings
Gifts

Talk to people who already have their own apartments. That way you can find out how much you might spend per month on these things. Discuss your needs for food and clothing costs with a counselor or with another parent.

To plan a budget, add up the cost each month of all items that are necessities. Then make a list of the optional items and what they cost. Subtract these totals from your expected monthly income.

It is important to be able to live on your income. If your basic expenses are less than your income, good. You can use the leftover money for your optional expenses and savings. Are your basic expenses greater than your income? Then you will need help.

Other Expenses

You need bedding, clothing, and feeding and bathing equipment for your baby. Fortunately, you can borrow many of these things or buy them second-hand.

Clothing   It will make your life easier to get simple, easy-to-handle clothing that fits loosely. Your baby will grow very quickly during the first year. So buy the 3- to 6-month size at first only if the baby is small.

  Diapers—4 dozen if you wash them yourself; a dozen "spares" if you use a diaper service; two dozen disposable diapers for day trips, visiting, etc.
  Tee Shirts—4–6
  Waterproof pants—3–4 (if you use only disposables, you won't need these)
  Sleepers—3–4 (sleeping "sacks," with a bottom tie or zipper, to keep baby's feet snug)
  Stretch suits—3–4
  Bibs
  Receiving blankets—3–4 (to keep your newborn baby snug and comfortable when going out)
  Sweaters—1–2
  Blanket sleeper
  Booties or socks
  Hat

  Outer clothing, such as snow suit (if you live where you'll need one)

Feeding Equipment   Breast feeding is generally more economical than feeding a baby formula. If you eat properly, your milk will be perfect food for your baby.

Bottles—if breast feeding, 2–3 for water and juice; if feeding formula, 8–9 (8-ounce size)
Mixing container marked in ounces (for formula)
Extra nipples
Bottle brush
Pot or kettle for sterilizing bottles

Bedding   You will not need a crib right away. In the beginning you can even use a box if you need to. Be sure it is cushioned for the baby to sleep in with soft padding. It is best *not* to use a pillow.

Crib and mattress
Mattress pads—2–3   Bumper
Waterproof sheets—2–3   Comforter
Fitted crib sheets—2–3

Bathing equipment   Plastic tub for bathing
Washcloths
Towels
Blunt-edged nail scissors
Petroleum jelly (vaseline)

Other equipment   Changing table
Diaper pail
Snuggler (tie-on carrier for baby that frees your hands and holds baby close to you)
Stroller
Auto safety seat

Chapter 9

Your New Role

The decision to become a mother is one of the most important that you will ever make. Raising a baby changes your life forever. It is important to understand the demands of parenting.

If you don't plan on having more children right away, you should see your midwife or doctor about getting birth control. You can become pregnant at any time.

This book has focused on having a child. It talked about the responsibilities of pregnancy and parenthood. These are your responsibilities if you decide to become a mother.

It is important to learn as much as you can about being a good mother. That means seeing counselors and medical professionals for your baby's health and well-being.

Like everything else, motherhood can be both good and bad. Having a baby limits your freedom. It can force you to grow up fast. Sometimes it can be expensive and frustrating. Becoming a mother when you are a teenager can be even more difficult.

At the same time, a baby can bring much joy to its mother. Even for teenagers, having a baby can change the mother's life for the better. Almost all mothers feel great love for their children. How you handle motherhood depends on you.

Glossary—*Explaining New Words*

antibodies   Cells produced by the body that can protect it from infection.
bonding   Feeling of closeness. Cuddling baby during feeding can help you bond.
bumper   Padded fabric that protects a baby's head from the crib's hard edges.
caesarian section   Surgical delivery of a baby.
cervix   Entryway to birth canal. Opens during childbirth.

childbirth   The process of having a baby.

colic   Sharp pains in a baby's intestines.

contraction   Squeezing and releasing of uterus to prepare for delivery of a baby.

embryo   Term for unborn baby during first trimester.

fetus   Term for unborn baby during last two trimesters.

fontanel   The soft spot on top of the baby's head.

formula   Liquid food used to feed baby. Available pre-made.

immunization   A shot that protects a person from a disease.

labor   First part of childbirth.

lochia   A bloody discharge after childbirth that can last for a week or more.

meconium   A dark greenish matter that appears in the first bowel movements of newborn infants.

midwife   Health care practitioner who specializes in delivering babies.

nutrients   Substances that promote growth and provide nutrition.

objective   Without previous opinions or judgments. For example, "A counselor at school is objective about your situation."

obstetrician   Doctor who specializes in childbirth.

pediatrician   Doctor who specializes in the care of babies.

placenta   Life support system for fetus in the uterus.

postnatal   After birth.

post-partum depression   Feeling of sadness after delivering baby.

prenatal   Before birth.

receiving blanket   Square of fabric used to wrap baby and for other purposes.

trimester   Each three months of pregnancy.

uterus   Muscular home for developing fetus.

Where To Go For Help

The following organizations can refer you to service groups in your area:

The Door, A Center for Alternatives
121 Avenue of the Americas
New York, New York 10013
(212) 941-9090

Family Service Association of America
11700 West Lake Park Drive
Park Place
Milwaukee, WI 53224
(414) 359-2111

Child Welfare League of America
440 First Street, N.W.
Washington, D.C. 20001
(202) 638-2952

Catholic Home Bureau
1011 First Avenue
New York, New York 10022
(212) 371-1000

Parents Anonymous
(800) 421-0353

The following organizations in your area may be
helpful. Look in the telephone book for more
information on:
  Maternity Services
  State Health Departments
  State Government (Ask for the Coordinator of
    Adolescent Pregnancy)
  Y.M.C.A., Y.W.C.A., and Y.M.H.A.
  The Red Cross
  Salvation Army

For Further Reading

Marks, Jane. "We Have A Problem." *Parents,* June, 1988, pages 58–65. This article discusses how one family handled their daughter's pregnancy and delivery.

Minor, Nancy and Patricia Bradley. *Coping with School Age Motherhood.* New York, NY: Rosen Publishing Group, Inc., 1988, 176 pages. This book tells the stories of many pregnant teenage girls and how they dealt with their situations.

Richards, Arlene Kramer and Irene Willis. *What To Do If Someone You Know Is Pregnant.* New York, NY: Lothrop, Lee & Shepard Books, 1983, 256 pages. This book discusses many issues involved in becoming a mother, including health care.

Spock, Dr. Benjamin and Dr. Michael B. Rothenberg. *Dr. Spock's Baby and Child Care.* New York, NY: Simon and Schuster, Inc., 740 pages. This is an excellent guide to caring for your baby.

Index

About the Author
Jane Hammerslough is a writer who has worked as a counselor to
teenagers, on family planning and other women's health issues. Ms.
Hammerslough is a graduate of Wesleyan University. She is married
and recently became a mother.

About the Editor
Evan Stark is a well-known sociologist, educator, and therapist
as well as a popular lecturer on women's and children's health issues.
Dr. Stark was the Henry Rutgers Fellow at Rutgers University, an as-
sociate at the Institution for Social and Policy Studies at Yale University, and a Fulbright Fellow at the University of Essex. He is the author
of many publications in the field of family relations and is the father of
four children.

Acknowledgments and Photo Credits
Photographs by Stuart Rabinowitz; p. 35, Sonja Kalter

Design/Production: Blackbirch Graphics, Inc.
Cover Photograph: Charles Waldron